THIS WALKER BOOK

For
RALPH
and the
NATURAL
THEATRE CO.

First published 1993 by
Walker Books Ltd
87 Vauxhall Walk, London SE11 5HJ

This edition published 1996

6 8 10 9 7 5

© 1993 Penny Dale

This book has been typeset in Bookman.

Printed in Hong Kong

British Library Cataloguing in Publication Data
A catalogue record for this book is
available from the British Library.

ISBN 0-7445-4383-5

TEN OUT OF BED

Penny Dale

Walker Books
AND SUBSIDIARIES
LONDON · BOSTON · SYDNEY

There were ten out of bed...

and the little one said, "Let's play!"

And Hedgehog said,
"Let's play TRAINS!"

So they all played trains
until Hedgehog fell asleep.

There were nine out of bed
and the little one said,
"Let's play!"

And Ted said,
"Let's play SEASIDES!"

So nine played seasides
until Ted fell asleep.

There were eight out of bed
and the little one said,
"Let's play!"

And Rabbit said,
"Let's play THEATRES!"

So eight played theatres
until Rabbit fell asleep.

There were seven out of bed
and the little one said,
"Let's play!"

And Bear said,
"Let's play PIRATES!"

So seven played pirates
until Bear fell asleep.

There were six out of bed
and the little one said,
"Let's play!"

And Sheep said,
"Let's play DANCING!"

So six played dancing
until Sheep fell asleep.

So five played ghosts
until Croc fell asleep.

So four played flying
until Nellie fell asleep.

There were three out of bed
and the little one said,
"Let's play!"

And Zebra said,
"Let's play CAMPING!"

So three played camping
until Zebra fell asleep.

There were two out of bed
and the little one said,
"Let's play!"

And Mouse said,
"Let's play MONSTERS!"

So two played monsters
until Mouse fell asleep.

There was one out of bed and the little one said,

"I'm sleepy now!"

So he slipped under the covers next to Ted.

Good night, sweet dreams, ten in the bed.

MORE WALKER PAPERBACKS
For You to Enjoy

Also illustrated by Penny Dale

TEN IN THE BED

"A subtle variation on the traditional nursery song,
illustrated with wonderfully warm pictures ...
crammed with amusing details." *Practical Parenting*

0-7445-1340-5   £4.99

BET YOU CAN'T!

"A lively argumentative dialogue – using simple,
repetitive words – between two children. Illustrated with
great humour and realism." *Practical Parenting*

0-7445-1225-5   £4.99

WAKE UP, MR B!

Commended for the Kate Greenaway Medal, this is the simple account
of a small girl playing some imaginative early morning games with her dog.

"Perceptive, domestic illustrations fill a varied cartoon-strip format ...
making this a lovely tell-it-yourself picture book." *The Good Book Guide*

0-7445-1467-3   £4.50

ROSIE'S BABIES

written by Martin Waddell

Winner of the Best Book for Babies Award
and shortlisted for the Kate Greenaway Medal.

"Deals with sibling jealousy in a very convincing way." *Child Education*

0-7445-2335-4   £4.99